T H E
APPALOOSA HORSE

by Gail B. Stewart

Illustrated with photographs
by William Muñoz

Reading consultant:

John Manning, Professor of Reading
University of Minnesota

Capstone Press

MINNEAPOLIS

Printed in the United States of America.

Capstone Press • 2440 Fernbrook Lane • Minneapolis, MN 554

Editorial Director   John Coughlan
Managing Editor   John Martin
Copy Editor   Gil Chandler

Library of Congress Cataloging-in-Publication Data

Stewart, Gail, 1949-
    The Appaloosa horse / by Gail B. Stewart.
        p. cm.
    Includes bibliographical references and index.
    ISBN 1-56065-243-8
    1. Appaloosa horse--Juvenile literature. [1. Appaloosa
    horse. 2. Horses.]   I. Title.
SF293.A7S84   1995
636.1'3--dc20   94-29980
                                            CIP
                                            AC

Table of Contents

Quick Facts about the Appaloosa Horse

Description

Height:	14.2 to 15.2 **hands** (equal to four-inch [ten-centimeter] segments) from the ground to the top of the shoulders. That works out to between 57 and 61 inches (140 and 150 centimeters) tall.
Weight:	950 to 1,175 lbs. (430 to 530 kilograms).
Physical features:	white rim (**sclera**) around the eye, black-and-white striped hooves, short mane, spotted pattern on coat, sloping shoulders, well-defined muscles.
Colors:	a variety of colors including black, white, brown, and reddish brown. There are five basic color patterns: **blanket**, snowflake, **leopard**, marble, and frost.

Development

History of breed:	Spanish horses specially bred for speed and color patterns by the **Nez Percés.**
Place of origin:	North America
Estimated number:	more than 450,000 pure Appaloosas are registered around the world, mostly in North America.

Food

Hay, grasses such as **timothy** and **clover**, grain
(especially oats and **bran**), and plenty of water. Every
day a full-grown Appaloosa horse needs about 14 pounds
(6 kilograms) of hay and grasses, between 4 and 12
quarts (3.8 and 11.3 liters) of oats and bran, and 12
gallons (45.5 liters) of water.

Life History

Life span: a well-cared-for Appaloosa may live
                      from 20 to 30 years.

Reproductive life: **stallions** are bred when they are about
                      two years old; **mares** when they are
                      three or four. Appaloosa mares carry
                      their **foals** for 11 months before
                      giving birth.

Uses

Appaloosas are used on cattle ranches for herding. They
are also used for rodeo and show events, as well as for
pleasure riding.

Chapter 1

A Look at the Appaloosa

The Appaloosa horse is impossible to miss
n a pasture, in a competition, or on a riding
rail. The spots on its coat look like blobs of
vhite, brown, and black paint. Its hooves are
vhite and black, like the stripes on a zebra.

"These horses are amazing," says horse
xpert Terry Kirby. "They are the most
eautiful horses in America. They are smart
nd gentle, too. They seem to understand what

want even before I give them instructions. I sometimes have to remind myself that they aren't human!"

A Strange History

This horse has an unusual history. In the late 1800s, the United States Army tried to trap and shoot the Appaloosas, even though the horses had done no harm. The Appaloosa horse survived, however, and became one of the most popular breeds in the world.

Where did the Appaloosa horse come from? Why did the United States Army consider it an enemy? And how did the horse survive such dangers?

Chapter 2

The Beginnings of the Appaloosa

There have been speckled and spotted horses since prehistoric times. About 20,000 years ago, cave dwellers made drawings of such horses. Horse owners in ancient China and Europe prized spotted horses because they were so unusual.

Coming to America

The horses which later became the Appaloosa breed came to America the same way all horses did–with the Spanish explorers.

The Spanish horses were stocky and strong animals called **jennets**. In Europe, the Spanish jennets were well-known for their speed and intelligence.

Horses and the Native Americans

When the Spanish came to the New World there were Native Americans already living in the woods and plains. The Indians were very interested in these spotted animals that they had never seen before. They saw how the Spanish tamed their horses and used them to herd cattle. They also saw how a man could hunt from the back of a horse.

As the years went by, Native Americans were able to get horses of their own. They captured some that were running free. They traded with the Spanish for others.

The Indians became skilled riders who could use their horses in battle or during a hunt. Many Indians enjoyed racing their horses, too.

The Nez Percés

One nation of Native Americans became very skilled in horsemanship. These were the Nez Percés, who lived in the northwestern part of what is now the United States.

The Nez Percés admired the speed and usefulness of horses. They also thought that horses were more than a tool for hunting or for

ransport. The Nez Percés believed that horses were gifts from the gods.

Over the years, these horses were named after the Palouse River, which flows through the Nez Percé lands. At first they were called "Palouses" or "Appalouseys." Eventually, the name became "Appaloosa."

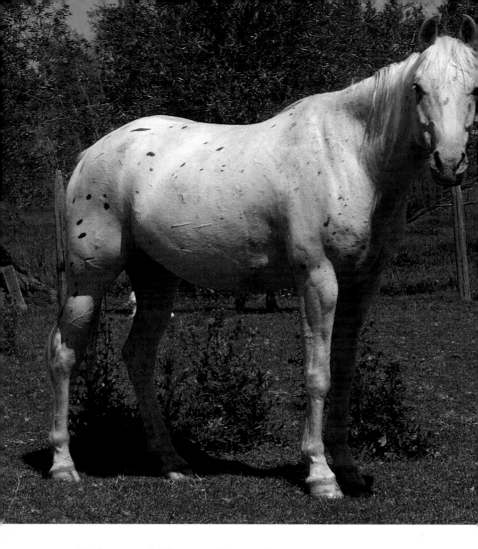

Talented Horse Breeders

The Nez Percés saw that young horses born to spotted parents were usually spotted, too. They took care to breed only the strongest and

16

most beautifully spotted horses. In this way
the Nez Percés improved the horses they
admired.

With each new generation, the spotted
horses of the Nez Percés became more
beautiful and spirited. Every horse was
different because the pattern of spots was
always different. A Nez Percé who owned one
of these horses was thought to be very lucky.

In 1805, the explorers Meriwether Lewis
and William Clark visited the Nez Percé
territory. The beauty of the Nez Percé horses
amazed them. The spotted horses were unlike
any horses they had ever seen.

Chapter 3

How the Appaloosa Almost Disappeared

The Appaloosa horse became the symbol of the Nez Percés. The sad fortune of this nation, however, would also mean bad things for the spotted horses.

Promises Broken

As white settlers traveled west in the 1850s and 1860s, they pushed many Native American people off their land. The Indians fought both the settlers and the U.S. Army. Many of the Nez Percés who survived the fighting were

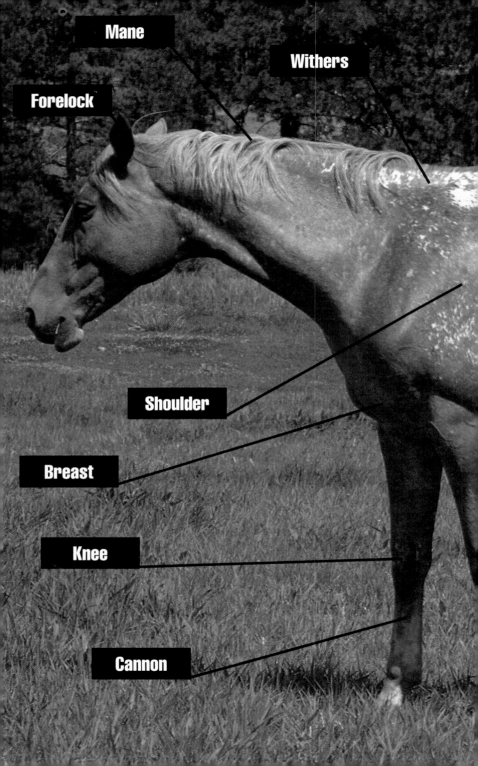

Mane

Withers

Forelock

Shoulder

Breast

Knee

Cannon

forced to move to government-run lands called
reservations.

Other Nez Percés were allowed to stay in
their homeland. They raised their beautiful
horses there and tried to get along with the
white settlers.

In 1877 the United States government
declared that it needed the Nez Percé land.
The Indians would have to move to a
reservation.

The leader of the Nez Percés, the famous Chief Joseph, felt betrayed. He fought back, and many of his people died in the battles that followed.

"I Will Fight No More Forever"

In one last effort to remain free, Chief Joseph led his people and their horses on an amazing journey. They headed north towards Canada and freedom. The United States Army chased the Indians through the mountains, but the Nez Percé horses kept going. Finally, however, their strength gave out–just 40 miles (64 kilometers) from Canada. Chief Joseph surrendered on October 5, 1877. In a sad speech, he said, "From where the sun now stands, I will fight no more forever."

The Nez Percés were forced to live on a reservation in Indian Territory (Oklahoma), far from their homeland. They had to give up the horses they loved so much. The army seized their Appaloosas, sold some of them, and shot those they couldn't sell.

"It was pure revenge," says one expert. "Why did our government destroy innocent animals? I think they did it to destroy the spirit of the Nez Percés. It was as though killing the horses was a way to kill the people, too. It was a very ugly part of history."

Horse on the Brink of Extinction

The people who bought the Appaloosas from the army did not breed the horses carefully, as the Indians had. Few of these new owners worried whether one Appaloosa was bred with another Appaloosa. Over the next 20 years, the breed almost disappeared.

By the beginning of the 20th century, there were fewer than 300 Appaloosa horses left.

Chapter 4

The Appaloosa Today

The story of the Appaloosa horse has a happy ending. In 1937 a student named Francis Haines wrote an article about the horses of the Nez Percés. He described the terrible things that had happened to the Indians and to their Appaloosa horses. Many people read his story and wanted to help save the spotted horses.

An Official Breed

In 1940 the Appaloosa Horse Club was established. Members of this club have worked hard to protect and improve the breed.

When the club began, only 22 Appaloosa horses were registered. Today there are more than 400,000 registered Appaloosas. The Appaloosa has become one of the world's most popular breeds. The horse that was nearly extinct has come back strong.

Physical Traits of the Appaloosa Horse

Not every horse with spots is an Appaloosa. But the breed is easy to recognize. According to the Appaloosa Horse Club, there are certain traits only Appaloosas have.

Appaloosa horses are not large. All horses are measured in hands, which are four-inch (10-centimeter) sections. A horse's height is measured from the **withers** (the spot at the top of the horse's shoulders) to the ground. Appaloosas stand between 14 hands, 2 inches (14 hands, 5 centimeters) and 15 hands, 2 inches (15 hands, 5 centimeters) tall.

Appaloosas have strong legs and are muscular. Their hooves, which are often zebra-striped, are so hard that the Appaloosa does not need horseshoes.

Their coat is different from that of other horses, too. Appaloosas have patches of what is called **mottled** (differently colored) hair on their coats. The skin under the coat of an Appaloosa has mixed colors, too. Light skin mixed with black appears around an Appaloosa's lips, its nostrils, its belly, and its rump.

One of the most interesting things about an Appaloosa is its eyes. Most horses–in fact, most animals–do not have white around the colored part of the eye. Their eyes are entirely black or brown. But the Appaloosa's eyes have a white part called a sclera. The sclera gives the eyes of Appaloosas the appearance of human eyes.

The Color Patterns of the Appaloosa

There are several color patterns among Appaloosas. One of the most common patterns is the "blanket." This is a patch of white over the hips. It looks as if someone had thrown a small white blanket over the horse. Sometimes the blanket has dark spots. Other times it is pure white.

A dark horse with white spots all over its body has a "snowflake" pattern. A "leopard" is a white horse with black or brown spots. Sometimes the spots of a leopard Appaloosa look like upside-down raindrops.

Appaloosas with the "marble" pattern have a dark coat when they're born. As the horse grows, the color fades almost to white. "Frost" is a dark pattern with light spots.

People who breed Appaloosas know that there is no way to predict the color pattern of a **foal** (baby horse). Even if both parents both have the frost pattern, for example, a foal could be born with a snowflake pattern or a leopard pattern.

To make things more confusing, the patterns of many Appaloosas change with age. Spots that are very clear at first can fade or disappear altogether. "Whatever you end up with," says one breeder, "is more luck than anything else. It's always a surprise!"

Chapter 5

The Appaloosa
in Action

There is much more to an Appaloosa horse than unusual colors and coats. They are gentle and very intelligent. This makes them a favorite horse for many different activities.

A woman who raises Appaloosas says, "Many horses seem to be just horses. But Appaloosas have a personality. One of them helped my husband build fences. The horse would pick up the wire and pull it on his own! He didn't do a very good job, of course, but at least he tried."

Since the Appaloosa became an official breed, there have been many opportunities for the spotted horses to enter competitions. Some of these contests are based on speed and agility. Others measure the horse's beauty and training. Whatever the event or contest, Appaloosas always add excitement to the show.

Horse Shows and Rodeos

Over the past several years, horse shows have been established just for Appaloosas. In these shows, judges look at each horse's body structure. They also judge how the horses trot and walk. The most beautiful and well-trained horses earn ribbons or trophies.

Some competitions require more speed and endurance than beauty. In the Nez Percé Stake Race, horses and their riders try to be the first to finish a tricky race course.

Before the race, officials set long stakes into the ground. Then two horses and riders race against one another, zigzagging back and forth

etween the stakes like skiers. The winner of
ne race competes against the winner of
nother, until every contestant has had a turn.
'he winner of the final race is the champion.

A Trail Ride Through History

One of the most interesting Appaloosa horse
vents honors the people who first bred the
orses, the Nez Percés. It is called the Chief
oseph Trail Ride, and it takes place each year
n August.

The ride follows the same trail Chief Joseph
sed to lead his people toward Canada in 1877.
ach year, Appaloosa horses and their owners
ome from all over North America to ride a
00-mile (160-kilometer) part of the journey.
'he next year, they cover another segment.
After 13 years, the entire 1300-mile journey
as been completed, and they start over.

The event is fun but also sad. One woman
as participated with her son for three years in
 row. "I had a very **eerie** feeling riding along
he same route the Indians had taken," she

explains. "We were riding horses who were descendants of the Nez Percé horses, and seeing the same cliffs and trees that Chief Joseph and his people had seen. It was a very moving experience for us."

A Horse with a Strong Spirit

No matter what Appaloosas do–horse shows, rodeo events, or pleasure riding–they d it with style. After nearly disappearing, the Appaloosa has returned. "This horse has a strong spirit," says one owner. "Not only is th Appaloosa horse beautiful on the outside, but i also has inner beauty and intelligence. It's impossible not to love these horses."

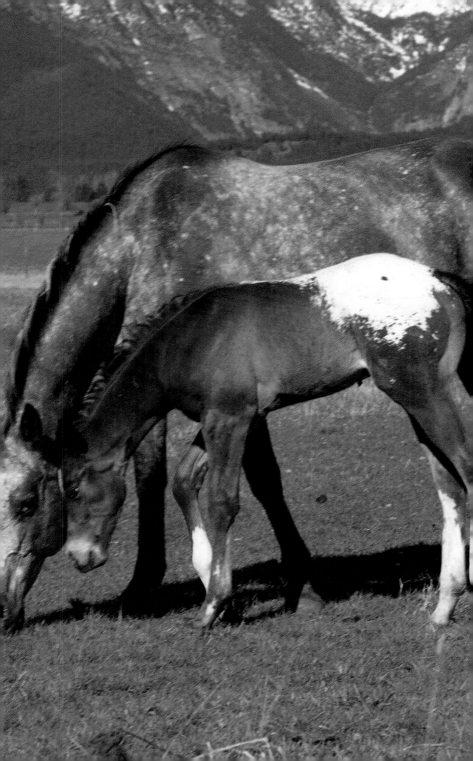

Glossary

blanket pattern–a white area on an Appaloosa horse's rump.

bran–a food for horses made from wheat

clover–a herb that horses eat

eerie–strange and frightening

foal–a baby horse

hands–four-inch (10-centimeter) segments. Horses all over the world are measured in hands.

jennet–a short, muscular Spanish horse brought to the New World in the 16th century

leopard pattern–dark spots on a white or light coat–a common pattern for Appaloosas

mare–a female horse

mottled–a spotted or differently colored skin around the nose, lips, belly, and rump of a horse

Nez Percés–a nation of Native Americans in the northwestern United States

Reservation–lands set aside by the U.S. government for Native Americans

Sclera–the white part of the eye surrounding the iris, or colored part

Stallion–a male horse

Timothy–a grass that horses eat

Withers–the top of a horse's shoulders

To Learn More

Balch, Glenn, *The Book of Horses*. New York:
Four Winds, 1967.

Brown, Fern G. *Horses and Foals*. New York:
Franklin Watts, 1986.

Henry, Marguerite. *Album of Horses*. New
York: Rand McNally, 1951.

Osinski, Alice. *The Nez Percé*. Chicago:
Childrens Press, 1988.

Patent, Dorothy Hinshaw. *Appaloosa Horses*.
New York: Holiday House, 1988.

Rifkin, Mark. *The Nez Percé Indians*. New
York: Chelsea House, 1994.

Self, Margaret Cabell. *The Complete Book of
Horses and Ponies*. New York: McGraw-
Hill, 1963.

You can read about Appaloosa horses in
these magazines: *Appaloosa Journal*, *Horse
Illustrated*, and *Horse and Rider*.

Some Useful Addresses

Appaloosa Horse Club and **Appaloosa Museum and Heritage Center**
P.O. Box 8403
Moscow, ID 83843

International Colored Appaloosa Association
P.O. Box 4424
Springfield, MO 65808-4424

Appaloosa Sport Horse Association
P.O. Box 160
Great Falls, VA 22066

Appaloosa Horse Club of Canada
P.O. Box 940
Claresholm, AB T0A 0T0

Index